A GUIDE TO
Quilling Flowers

Helen Walter

SALLYMILNER
PUBLISHING

First published in 2002 by
Sally Milner Publishing Pty Ltd
PO Box 2104
Bowral NSW 2576
AUSTRALIA

© Helen Walter 2002
Reprinted 2003

Design by Anna Warren, Warren Ventures Pty Ltd
Edited by Anne Savage
Photography by Tim Connolly

Printed in China

National Library of Australia Cataloguing-in-Publication data:
Walter, Helen.
  A guide to quilling flowers.

  ISBN 1 86351 306 X.

  1. Paper quillwork. 2. Paper quillwork — Patterns. I.
  Title. (Series : Milner craft series).

745.54

10 9 8 7 6 5 4 3 2

Contents

Introduction

It seemed at first glance a considerable challenge to find flowers suitable to interpret through the medium of quilling, but I was encouraged by the results of my early efforts to create new designs drawing on the vast resources that nature has to offer. This great country of Australia is a paradise of native floral beauty, with the climate also well suited to many exotic species from other parts of the world.

I have spent many hours poring over various flower publications, many more studying flowers in the wild and in my garden. In several instances flowers which I was sure would be simple to quill (they looked great in the photo!) turned out looking dull and boring. I have quite a collection of 'failures', designs which I felt did not live up to their original inspiration, yet other flowers that I thought would be impossible turned out to be most effective.

I hope that other quillers will be inspired to go beyond the designs offered here, to look more closely at the flowers around them, whether in their own backyards, a botanical garden or a nature reserve, and view them with quilling shapes in mind to come up with their own unique interpretations of local plant life.

Notes

Unless specified otherwise, all designs use 3 mm (1/8") quilling papers.

A standard size blank card (11 x 15 cm/ 4 1/2 x 6") has been used to display all the quilled wildflower designs. I have used cream or white cards for uniformity of presentation but many, especially the paler coloured flowers, would also look spectacular on a dark background.

Quilled cards can be posted! Just cut a piece of bubble wrap to fit over your design before placing it in the envelope. Make sure you keep the quilled part away from where the stamp will go. Some of the more built-up designs may need to be packaged in a small box, however, as they are too thick to fit into an envelope without being damaged.

Basic quilling equipment

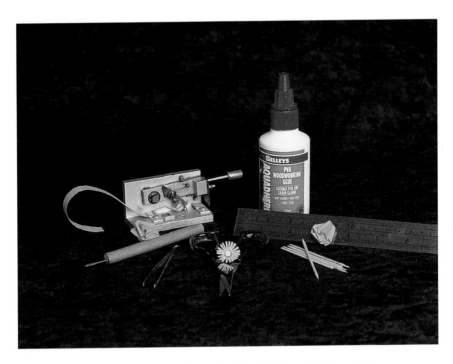

Quilling is a simple, portable and affordable craft. Expensive equipment is not required, and you don't need a lot of room to work in. You will need the following equipment to make any of the designs shown in this book.

Quilling papers of varying widths

The most commonly used papers are 3 mm (1/8"), 4 mm (3/16"), 6 mm (1/4") and 10 mm (1/2") wide. They are available from most craft suppliers.

Slotted quilling tool

This tool is used for coiling the strips of quilling paper. If you are handy it is a simple task to make your own tool from a 10 cm (4") length of dowelling wood and a tapestry needle. Insert the pointed end of the needle firmly into one end of the dowel and then nip off the very end of the eye with a pair of pliers to create the slot. To purchase a ready-made tool ask your local craft supplier.

Tweezers

These are available from the supermarket or pharmacy. Flat-jawed tweezers are the best. They are used to hold the quilled shape while you apply the glue, and for placing the glued shapes into position on the card.

Scissors

I find small pointed scissors are most useful. They must be sharp.

Ruler or tape measure

Used to measure the lengths of quilling paper specified.

Toothpicks

These are available at supermarkets. Use them to apply the glue to the quilled shape.

White PVA glue

Several brands are available from craft shops, hardware stores or newsagents. The clear-drying sort is a must. Only a small amount is needed.

Blank cards

White or coloured blank cards can be purchased from craft shops or printer's suppliers.

Fringing tool

Many of these designs include fringed parts and a fringing tool will make the job much easier. Cutting even slits with scissors becomes very tedious! They may be purchased through most craft suppliers.

Basic quilling techniques

Measure the length of quilling paper required, then tear or cut it to length. Slide one end of the paper into the slot of the quilling tool and wind it to make a coil. For a tight coil apply glue to the end while it is still on the tool.

For a loose coil take the coiled paper off the tool and place it on the desk in front of you, allowing it to loosen a little before glueing the end. Use your fingers to squeeze the loose coils to the required shape.

Hold the finished quilled shape or strip with the tweezers, apply glue with the toothpick, then place on the card in the required position.

Double-fringing technique

I have introduced double fringing for several of the flowers in this book. To do this you simply run the strip of quilling paper through your fringing tool twice to produce a much finer, more feathery fringe. You will need to use a good-quality paper, as the thinner papers don't feed through the fringing tool as well the second time.

Basic quilled shapes

Tight coil

Wind a strip into a coil, then without allowing it to unwind glue the end of the strip while the coil is still on the tool.

Teardrop

Make a loose coil and pinch one side to a point to resemble a teardrop shape.

Loose coil

Wind a tight coil and take it off the tool, allowing it to loosen before glueing the end of the strip.

Bent teardrop

Make a teardrop shape and bend the pinched end.

Eye

Make a loose coil and pinch the opposite sides evenly to resemble an eye.

Diamond

Make an eye and then push fingers together to make a diamond shape.

Leaf

Make a loose coil and pinch into an eye shape, then bend the pinched ends in opposite directions.

Triangle

Make a loose coil and pinch the three corners to make a triangle shape.

Arrow

Make a loose coil and pinch to a triangle shape. Pinch two corners firmly to form an arrow shape.

Half moon

Make a loose coil and pinch two points to make one flat side and one rounded side.

Crescent

Make a loose coil and pinch two points, bending the coil to make a crescent moon.

Beehive

Roll a tight coil into a cone shape and glue the end before taking it off the tool.

Birdfoot

Make a loose coil and shape into a triangle. Bend all three points in the same direction and squeeze firmly.

Star

Roll a loose coil and pinch five points evenly around it to make a star shape.

How to make rose flowers

Step 1: Take a 20 cm (7 3/4") strip of 10 mm (1/2") wide paper and place one end into the slot of the quilling tool.

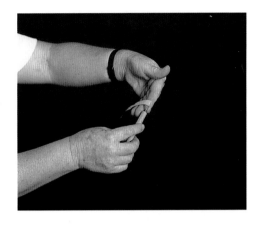

Step 2: Roll three turns on the tool and put on a spot of glue to hold in place.

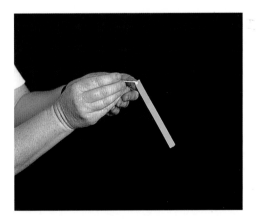

Step 3: Fold the paper towards you at a right angle and roll, allowing the top edge to flare out but keeping the bottom edge firmly against the tool.

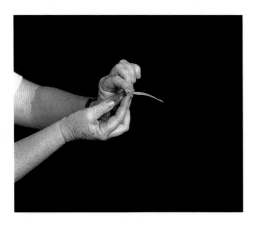

Step 4: Add a spot of glue to hold, and continue to fold and roll the paper, glueing at every turn until you reach the end of the paper strip.

Step 5: Fold the end of the strip under the rose and glue to hold in place. Leave the rose on the tool until it can be removed without unravelling. You may need to add a few more dabs of glue in strategic places! Your rose is complete.

How to make a fringed flower

Step 1: Measure and cut the lengths of plain and fringed quilling papers specified in the design. Glue the pieces end to end in the prescribed order to make a long strip of paper.

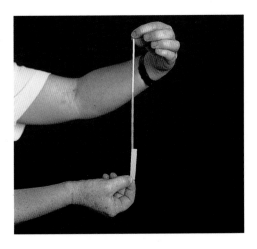

Step 2: Allow the glue to dry for a few moments, then insert the plain end into the slot of the quilling tool and commence to roll into a tight coil.

Step 3: Glue the end while the coil is still on the tool. Allow to dry for a few moments.

Step 4: Remove from tool and gently spread fringes with your fingertips. Your fringed flower is complete.

Twiners and climbers

Among the many and varied types of flowers on offer in Australia, there are surprisingly few native climbers, limited to membership of a very few species. In the wild these lianas creep, twine, ramble, climb and cascade over the surrounding undergrowth. While most of them occur in the southern forests, some don't mind a warmer climate, and nearly all of them have adapted well to cultivation. It is not unusual to see climbers native to this country growing in domestic situations both here and overseas, over sheds, fences and outhouses, together with imported Jasmine and Wisteria, Bougainvillea and Passionfruit. Their purple, red, orange, white and pink blooms brighten up the depths of the forests and drape a dignified mantle over rickety wooden pergolas.

WARRINE
Dioscorea hastifolia

This rather delicate climber is quite prolific throughout the mid-west of Western Australia. It is one of the earliest plants to show new life after the introductory autumn rains, with tendrils of green quickly twining up and through the trunks and branches of the surrounding brown scrub, followed by little strings of pale yellow flowers. Warrine is also known as the Native Yam. There are three tropical species of Dioscorea; the roots of these are edible, but only after grinding and washing to remove toxins.

Part	Quantity	Length	Shape	Colour
Flowers	63	3 cm (1 1/4")	tight coil	lemon
Stems	1	12 cm (4 3/4")	strip	mid-green
	8	2 cm (3/4")	strip	lemon
Leaves	6	15 cm (6")	teardrop	mid-green

ARRANGEMENT

Position main green stem onto card as illustrated and glue down. Place the short lemon stems coming off the main stem. Glue the tight coils along the short stems, one at the end of each, and four or five down either side. Squeeze the green teardrops quite firmly to make thin, slightly curved leaves and glue into position along the main stem.

CORAL VINE
Kennedia coccinea

The Coral Vine is a dainty yet vigorous creeper that runs rampant over anything that gets in its way, and when in full bloom gives the bush the appearance of being on fire. It is prolific, particularly in the Jarrah forests in the south-west of Western Australia. Flowers are made up of different hues of orange, pink and yellow, giving an overall massed effect of flames leaping across the undergrowth. Other Kennedia species produce mainly red flowers, with the exception of Kennedia nigricans which has black and yellow blooms.

Part	Quantity	Length	Shape	Colour
Flowers	14	10 cm (4")	half moon	orange
	14	5 cm (2")	crescent	purple
	14	2 cm (3/4")	tight coil	yellow
Buds	4	5 cm (2")	teardrop	orange
Stems	1	28 cm (11")	strip	mid-green
	5	3 cm (1 1/4")	strip	mid-green
	17	0.5 cm (1/4")	strip	mid-green
Leaves	14	10 cm (4")	teardrop	mid-green

To construct each flower, insert a yellow tight coil just inside the first coil on the flat side of the orange half moon. The springiness of the coil should keep it in position but if it falls out a spot of glue will hold it. Take a purple crescent and glue it to the orange half moon on the flat side, as you see in the photograph.

ARRANGEMENT

Curve the long green strip into an S-shape for the main stem and glue onto card. Position and glue the 3 cm (1 1/4") stems coming upwards off the main stem. From the top of each of these stems, radiating downwards, glue on two or three 0.5 cm (1/4") stems. At the end of each stem position a flower or bud.

WILD SARSAPARILLA
Hardenbergia comptoniana

Also known as Native Wisteria, this vigorous and hardy creeper is found throughout the southern Karri and Jarrah forests of Western Australia. In the wild it has mauve-blue flowers which spill over the surrounding understorey in a careless fashion. It has been widely cultivated as far away as Mozambique and Madagascar, and is popular in both suburban and country gardens. Wild Sarsaparilla is ideal for covering unsightly walls and fences, and cultivated blooms come in a range of white, pink or purple shades.

Part	Quantity	Length	Shape	Colour
Flowers	9	10 cm (4")	half moon	deep mauve
	9	5 cm (2")	crescent	deep mauve
	9	2 cm (3/4")	tight coil	white
Buds	2	5 cm (2")	teardrop	deep mauve
Stem	1	11 cm (4 3/8")	strip	mid-green
Leaves	3	18 cm (7 1/16")	teardrop	mid-green

To construct each flower, insert a white tight coil just inside the first coil on the flat side of the mauve half moon. The springiness of the coil should keep it in position but if it falls out a spot of glue will hold it. Take a mauve crescent and glue it to a mauve half moon on the flat side as shown.

ARRANGEMENT

Position the stem hanging downwards from the top of the card. Glue the buds to the tip of the stem. Place flowers either side of the stem almost opposite each other and glue in position. Lastly add leaves near the top of the stem.

TWINING FRINGED LILY
Thysanotus patersonii

This twining perennial is widespread across all states of Australia. The flowers appear to be sun sensitive, closing up on dull days and at night. It was named by the famed botanist Robert Brown, born in Scotland on 21 December 1773. Although he originally studied for the medical profession and joined the military in this capacity, his main interest was botany. When he was offered the position of naturalist on the 1801 survey of the then little-known coasts of New Holland under Captain Matthew Flinders, he jumped at it. When the expedition returned in 1805 Brown brought with him almost 4000 species of dried plants, many of them new. Despite being the foremost botanist of the day and the recipient of many awards and honours for his contributions to botanical science, Brown remained a very private and reserved individual virtually unknown to those outside the field of botany. He died at the age of 85 on 10 June 1858.

Part	Quantity	Length	Shape	Colour
Flowers	12	8 cm (3 1/4")	strip	violet
	12	3 cm (1 1/4")	double-fringed 6 mm strip	violet
	12	8 cm (3 1/4")	eye	violet
Stem	1	25 cm (9 3/4")	strip	mid-green
Leaves	2	15 cm (6")	teardrop	mid-green

To make the fringed flower petals glue each 8 cm (3 1/4")violet strip to a 3 cm (1 1/4") double-fringed 6 mm (1/4") violet strip. Commencing at the plain end, roll into a loose coil. The fringe should go around the coil only once with no overlap. Gently squeeze into an eye shape.

ARRANGEMENT

Curve stem into an irregular S-shape and glue to card. Each flower needs three fringed eyes and three plain eyes, glued into place as illustrated. Add the two leaves after squeezing them firmly to make them thin and slightly curved.

BOUGAINVILLEA
Bougainvillea spp.

Bougainvilleas are not classified as vines, rather they are climbing shrubs. They look fantastic rambling over fences and pergolas which provide the much-needed support for their long branching stems. Although they originate in the tropics, bougainvilleas also thrive in the hot dry subtropics and in many temperate zones, and will flower profusely after a dry season. The flamboyantly colourful bracts can be magenta, mauve, white, orange, crimson or pink. The foliage can be plain or variegated. Beware of the thorns—on some varieties they can be long and vicious. Bougainvilleas can be kept under control by being planted in a large container. They are named after Louis de Bougainville (1729–1811), a French navigator.

Part	Quantity	Length	Shape	Colour
Flower	13	15 cm (6")	diamond	purple
	1	5 cm (2")	tight coil	white
You will need to make 9 flowers altogether.				
Leaves	2	10 cm (4")	teardrop	green
	9	20 cm (7 3/4")	teardrop	green
Stems	1	14 cm (5 1/2")	strip	green
	1	12 cm (4 3/4")	strip	green

To construct the first flower, glue together three purple diamonds with points and sides touching so they form an upside down pyramid shape. You may need to hold this carefully until it is dry so it doesn't come apart. Glue a white tight coil into the centre. Follow this procedure for the other eight flowers.

ARRANGEMENT

Glue the two stems to the card so they look as though they're hanging down from the top left corner. Take the two small leaves and put one at the end of each stem. Add the remaining leaves along the stems. Group the flowers along the stem as desired.

PASSIONFLOWER
Passiflora caerulea

While this design rates an 8 out of 10 on the degree-of-difficulty scale (it is fiddly to get all the little stigma bits stuck on the top without them falling off), the finished effect is well worth the effort. Definitely a card for a very special person. The Passionflower is native to South America and was named by the early missionaries to that continent. To them it symbolised Christ's crucifixion. The ten petals were the ten faithful apostles, the purple and white rays of the corona were the crown of thorns, the five anthers were the five wounds, the three stigmas were the nails. The twining tendrils of the vine were the whips and the leaves were the hands of Christ's persecutors. The missionaries were convinced that the flower was a sign from heaven that their mission would be successful.

Part	Quantity	Length	Shape	Colour
Flower 1	10	12 cm (4 3/4")	eye	white
	1	10 cm (4")	fringed 10 mm strip	white
	1	15 cm (6")	fringed 6 mm strip	purple
	1	10 cm (4")	10 mm strip	lime green
	5	1 cm (1/2")	tight coil	lime green
	5	1 cm (1/2")	tight coil	yellow
	3	3 cm (1 1/4")	1.5 mm strip	purple

Flower 2 is the same as flower 1.

Leaf 1	3	15 cm (6")	eye	green

Leaves 2, 3, 4, 5 and 6 are the same as leaf 1.

Stem	1	20 cm (7 3/4")	strip	green
Leaf stems	7	1.5 cm (5/8")	strip	green

To construct the flower, first study the photograph! Take the 10 cm (4")) fringed white 10 mm (1/2") strip, the 15 cm (6") fringed purple 6 mm (1/4") strip and the 10 cm (4") green 10 mm (1/2") strip and glue them together end to end to make a 35 cm (13 7/8") strip that is white, purple and green. Starting from the plain green end, roll into a tight coil and glue. Do not spread the fringes out yet. Take the 10 white eyes and glue them evenly around the base of the fringed tight coil. When dry, gently spread out the white fringes and some of the purple fringes.

Glue the five lime-green tight coils to the five yellow tight coils to make five T-shapes. Glue the green ends of the T-shapes to the top of the green centre of the fringed coil so they radiate outward.

Roll the three purple 1.5 mm (1/16") strips into tight coils, leaving a 3 mm (1/8") section uncoiled at the end. Position the coils on top of the green centre of the fringed coil. Glue the uncoiled ends together and insert into the centre so the coils are raised above the rest of the flower.

To construct the leaves position three green eyes side by side and glue the bottom halves together.

Arrangement

Glue the main stem to the card in a curving shape so it looks like a vine. Attach short stems to it. Place a leaf at the top of the main stem, the remaining leaves and the flowers at the end of each short stem. Glue into place.

Succulents and cacti

Botanically speaking, succulents are those plants with fleshy and juicy leaves. They are also generally hardy, drought and salt tolerant. Not for them the pampered life of an indoor house plant or balcony dweller—though of course the more exotic succulents and cacti lap up this kind of attention.

Succulents and cacti are the camels of the plant world as often the plants continue to thrive, flowering and seeding by virtue of the moisture stored in their leaves long after the soil has dried out, just like a camel can draw on the reserves of fat stored in its hump to survive during dry periods.

The succulents and cacti that grow in the wild are varied in the shape, colour and size of their flowers, leaves and spines, and add a different dimension to the floral landscape.

ROUND-LEAVED PIGFACE
Disphyma crassifolium

Pigface is one of those plants that everyone knows about but doesn't pay much attention to. There are a few different types, varying in both the shape of the leaf and the colour of the flower. It grows readily even under quite harsh conditions, and has adapted well to cultivation, conveniently filling in that no-man's-land spot in the back (or front) yard. Although its succulent leaves look juicy and inviting to animals, it is in fact too salty for them to eat. Why it is called Pigface is anybody's guess, as I can't see the slightest resemblance to a pig.

Part	Quantity	Length	Shape	Colour
Flowers	6	15 cm (6")	strip	white
	6	2 cm (3/4")	fringed 4 mm strip	white
	6	2 cm (3/4")	fringed 10 mm strip	lilac
Stems	1	12 cm (4 3/4")	strip	brown
	1	14 cm (5 1/2")	strip	brown
Leaves	8	5 cm (2")	teardrop	brown
	40	5 cm (2")	teardrop	green

To construct each flower, make a 19 cm (7 1/2") length by glueing together a 15 cm (6") white strip, a 2 cm (3/4") white fringed 4 mm (3/16") strip, and a 2 cm (3/4") lilac fringed 10 mm (1/2") strip. Starting at the plain white end, roll into a tight coil and glue. When dry, gently spread the fringed part outwards with your fingers.

ARRANGEMENT

Glue stems into position on the card. Glue a green leaf at the tip of each stem and then continue with the rest of the leaves in pairs on each side of the stem, adding in the brown leaves and flowers as you wish, until both stems are fully covered.

YELLOW SALT-STAR
Gunniopsis intermedia

Stars have been a major influence on humanity for thousands of years. The sun, which gives us warmth, light (and skin cancer), is in fact a star. Sailors have used stars to navigate and plot their course by ever since the invention of the canoe. The Wise Men followed a star to Bethlehem. Stars are a feature on the flags of many nations. Great actors and singers are known as stars. A blow on the head or a feeling of faintness can cause a person to 'see stars'. Stars feature prominently in poetry and song, often in relation to wishing and hopes for the future. How many of you know your mother-in-law's star sign, but not the exact date of her birthday? The word 'star' is used in the names of plants and animals, often describing its shape or markings. Among these are starfish, star finches and starflowers. The Yellow Salt-Star is thus named, an apt reference to the shape of its fleshy flowers and its favoured habitat on the margins of salt lakes in the inland Goldfields and Wheatbelt areas of Western Australia.

Part	Quantity	Length	Shape	Colour
Flowers	3	5 cm (2")	strip	yellow
	3	2 cm (3/4")	fringed 10 mm (1/2") strip	lemon
	12	15 cm (6")	teardrop	yellow
Stems	5	assorted	strip	sage green
Leaves	12	8 cm (3 1/4")	eye	sage green

To form the flower centres join together a 5 cm (2") yellow strip and a 2 cm (3/4") lemon fringed 10 mm (1/2") strip. Starting at the plain yellow end, roll into a tight coil and glue. Spread the fringes only slightly when the glue is dry.

ARRANGEMENT

Decide on your arrangement, then glue one flower into position, starting with the centre and then adding four yellow teardrops around it as the petals. Add a stem and put the next flower at the end of it. Continue until all flowers and stems are in place. Add leaves last.

SEA-URCHIN CACTUS
Astrophytum asterias

Sea-urchin cacti fit into the category of pampered succulents in Australia. They are native to Mexico, but are very popular with cactus-lovers in other parts of the world. This sea-urchin cactus resembles its ocean-dwelling namesake in shape, but unlike the real sea urchin has no spines. It flowers in summer and can grow to a height of 8 cm (3 1/4") and a width of 10 cm (4").

Part	Quantity	Length	Shape	Colour
Flower 1	1	4 cm (1 1/2")	6 mm fringed strip	yellow
	1	20 cm (7 3/4")	strip	orange
		10 cm (4")	10 mm (1/2") fringed strip	yellow

Flowers 2 and 3 are the same as flower 1.

Part	Quantity	Length	Shape	Colour
Cactus body	8	30 cm (11 3/4")	triangle	green
	1	60 cm (23 1/4")	beehive	green
	32	3 cm (1 1/4")	1.5 mm (1/16") tight coil	white

To construct each flower make a 34 cm (13 5/8") length by glueing together the 4 cm (1 1/2") yellow fringed 6 mm (1/4") strip, the 20 cm (7 3/4") orange strip, and the 10 cm (4") yellow fringed 10 mm (1/2") strip. Starting at the short yellow fringed end, roll into a tight coil and glue. When dry, gently spread the outer fringed part only outwards with your fingers.

To make the body of the cactus glue the triangles side by side to form a roughly circular shape. It doesn't matter if the middle isn't neat, it will be covered by the flowers. Glue on the white tight coils, one on the outer edge of each triangle and three on the top of each triangle in a line.

ARRANGEMENT

Take the 60 cm (23 1/4") green beehive, making sure it is only a shallow cone in shape. Glue this to the centre of your card with the pointed end up. Take the cactus body and glue it centrally on top of the cone, making sure that the edge is stuck to the card all the way round. The cactus should now be cone-shaped. Glue the three fringed flowers on top of the cactus, covering any gaps. Using a paintbrush, spread some glue on the card around the cactus and sprinkle with fine sand. Shake off excess sand. Your cactus is now in the desert!

PARAKEELYA
Calandrinia polyandra

The flowers of this pretty little succulent are open for only one day. They open early in the morning, and are often closed and finished by the middle of the afternoon. Their deep pink petals provide a bright splash of colour around the edges of claypans, granite boulders and gnamma holes (depressions in the ground, usually in rock, forming natural reservoirs for rainwater). The leaves of Parakeelya, which resemble mini jelly-beans, are quite juicy and edible. Sheep love Parakeelya, but eating excessive amounts of it can be a problem for the males, as it can lead to the formation of urinary stones which block the urethra, potentially (though fortunately not commonly) leading to a rupture of the bladder for which there is no known cure.

Part	Quantity	Length	Shape	Colour
Flowers	25	12 cm (4 3/4")	teardrop	deep pink
	5	2 cm (3/4")	strip	white
	5	8 cm (3 1/4")	strip	yellow
Buds	4	8 cm (3 1/4")	teardrop	deep pink
Stems	1	10 cm (4")	strip	brown
	2	8 cm (3 1/4")	strip	brown
	2	4 cm (1 1/2")	strip	brown
	4	1 cm (1/2")	strip	brown
Leaves	9	5 cm (2")	teardrop	brown

To make the flower centre, join together a white 2 cm (3/4") strip and a yellow 8 cm (3 1/4") strip to make a 10 cm (4") strip. Starting at the white end, roll into a tight coil and glue.

ARRANGEMENT

Place flower centres randomly on card. Arrange five pink 12 cm (4 3/4") teardrops around each flower centre and glue into position. Add stems, then the leaves and buds, as illustrated in the photograph.

PRICKLY PEAR
Opuntia vulgaris

Ouch!! The spines of the Prickly Pear are vicious, which is one of the reasons that the plant is used in different parts of the world as a hedge or fence. No creature dares to climb through. In Australia the Prickly Pear is considered a noxious weed, but in other countries it ranks highly, both as an edible fruit and as cattle fodder. Removing the spines is the tricky bit, but then the fruits can be made into jam or jelly, or just eaten raw. Cattle don't like the prickles much either, but in times of drought farmers cut or burn off the spines so that the cattle can enjoy the juicy green leaves.

Part	Quantity	Length	Shape	Colour
Flowers	18	10 cm (4")	beehive	red
Leaves	1	60 cm (23 1/4")	teardrop	green
	2	45 cm (17 3/4")	teardrop	green
	2	30 cm (11 3/4")	teardrop	green
Spines	30	0.5 cm (1/4")	10 mm (1/2") fringed strip	cream
Ground	1	8 cm (3 1/4")	strip	brown

To make the spines roll each of the 0.5 cm (1/4") cream fringed 10 mm (1/2")strips into a tight coil.

ARRANGEMENT

Place the brown strip for the ground along the bottom of the card and glue into place. Starting with the largest leaf at the bottom, position the leaves on the card and glue down. Add the flowers and spines as desired.

Native garden favourites

Everyone is much more conscious these days about the need to conserve water. Water is a precious commodity in many parts of the world, some regions relying on hundreds of kilometres of pipeline to supply them with the precious liquid. Many introduced plants require a lot of water and, faced with Australia's summer heat, simply frizzle up and die. More and more people are turning to utilising native plants instead to bring beauty and variety to their gardens. Many native species are rich in nectar and this of course attracts honey-loving birds, another plus. Commercial flower producers have also become interested in native varieties, since there is a demand overseas for Australian cut wildflowers.

GERALDTON WAX

Chamelaucium uncinatum

In the wild, Geraldton Wax grows along the western coastline between Perth and Geraldton, and the flowers are a pale pink. Now widely cultivated, and available in shades of purple, pink and white, it is popular with home gardeners, especially those contending with sandy soils. Unfortunately, because of its adaptability it is beginning to encroach into National Parks in some areas, and runs the risk of becoming a pest. It is long lasting as a cut flower, and is an important income-earner for commercial wildflower growers, being much sought after overseas.

Part	Quantity	Length	Shape	Colour
Flowers	7	15 cm (6")	strip	salmon pink
	7	2 cm (3/4")	fringed 4 mm (3/16") strip	white
	35	10 cm (4")	teardrop	white
Stems	1	10 cm (4")	strip	dark green
	2	3 cm (1 1/4")	strip	dark green
	4	2 cm (3/4")	strip	dark green
Leaves	20	1 cm (1/2")	strip	dark green

To construct each flower centre, make a 17 cm (6 3/4") length by glueing together a 15 cm (6") salmon-pink strip and a 2 cm (3/4") white fringed 4 mm (3/16") strip. Starting at the plain salmon-pink end, roll into a tight coil and glue. When dry, gently spread the fringed part slightly outwards with your fingers.

ARRANGEMENT

Position and glue the 10 cm (4") main stem onto the card. Place a flower centre at the end of the stem. Then take five of the white 10 cm (4") teardrops and arrange them evenly around the centre, points touching the centre, before glueing. Position the remaining stems and repeat the process, putting a flower at the end of each stem. Add the 1 cm strips for leaves, curving each one slightly.

SWAN RIVER DAISY

Brachyscome iberidifolia

Daisies have been an integral part of flower gardens around the world for hundreds of years and the daisy family, Asteraceae, is one of the largest in the world. Children have long learnt the art of making daisy-chains, and how many of us in our youth have carefully picked off the petals, chanting 'he-loves-me, he-loves-me-not'. Daisies are so adaptable that they are regarded as weeds in many places. The Swan River Daisy was a hit with European gardeners as early as 1830. With its white, blue, pink, or purple flowers, it is a popular addition to many gardens today, especially as a rockery plant.

Part	Quantity	Length	Shape	Colour
Flowers	6	15 cm (6")	strip	yellow
	6	2 cm (3/4")	fringed 10 mm (1/2") strip	white
Stems	6	assorted	strip	green
Leaves	14	5 cm (2")	bent teardrop	green

To construct each flower, make a 17 cm (6 3/4") length by glueing together a 15 cm (6") yellow strip and a 2 cm (3/4") white fringed 10 mm (1/2") strip. Starting at the plain yellow end, roll into a tight coil and glue. When dry, gently spread the fringed part outwards with your fingers.

ARRANGEMENT

Commencing with the stems, arrange them radiating out from a central point. Glue a flower at the end of each stem. Add the leaves, making sure the pointed end touches the stem.

LESSER BOTTLEBRUSH
Callistemon phoeniceus

Of all the bottlebrushes to be found in Australia, only two species are indigenous to Western Australia. This gorgeous fiery-red specimen dazzles the senses with its big red brushes throughout spring and early summer. It is very hardy and a popular addition to the home garden. Callistemons like to be pruned after flowering, and will also respond to a well-balanced fertiliser. Honeyeaters love bottlebrushes too and are a sight to behold, hanging almost upside down to get every last drop of nectar from the weeping blooms.

Part	Quantity	Length	Shape	Colour
Flowers	19	5 cm (2")	strip	red
	19	8 cm (3 1/4")	fringed 10 mm (1/2") strip	red
Stems	1	11 cm (4 1/4")	strip	brown
Leaves	1	30 cm (11 3/4")	bent teardrop	mid-green
	1	20 cm (7 3/4")	bent teardrop	mid-green
	3	15 cm (6")	bent teardrop	mid-green

To construct each flower, make a 13 cm (5 1/4") length by glueing together a 5 cm (2") red strip and an 8 cm (3 1/4") red fringed 10 mm (1/2") strip. Starting at the plain end, roll into a tight coil and glue. When dry, gently spread the fringed part outwards with your fingers.

ARRANGEMENT

Position the stem hanging in a downwards curve. Take 12 of the flowers and glue them on their sides in 6 pairs opposite each other on either side of the stem. Take the remaining seven flowers and glue them on top of the stem and paired flowers as illustrated. Place two of the 15 cm (6") leaves at the top end of the flowering stem, and the remaining leaves at the other end, curving upwards a little.

RAPIER FEATHERFLOWER
Verticordia mitchelliana

Named after Sir James Mitchell KCMG, a former Premier of Western Australia, this featherflower is one of the easiest of the species to grow in cultivation. The rapier-like style is almost four times as long as the rest of the flower, and worthy of many a duel. Unlike most other plants, the flowers of this species hang upside down under the leaves of the bush. The brilliant red of the flowers is especially prominent against the grey-green background of the leaves and the various coloured sands in which it likes to grow.

Part	Quantity	Length	Shape	Colour
Flowers	7	20 cm (7 3/4")	strip	red
	7	4 cm (1 1/2")	double-fringed 10 mm (1/2") strip	red
	7	3 cm (1 1/4")	sliver	red
Stems	3	5 cm (2")	strip	grey
Leaves	5	15 cm (6")	eye	sage green
	10	20 cm (7 3/4")	eye	sage green

To construct each flower, make a 24 cm (9 1/2") length by glueing together a 20 cm (7 3/4") red strip and a 4 cm (1 1/2") red double-fringed 10 mm (1/2") strip. Starting at the plain end, roll into a beehive and glue. Remove from the quilling tool and with a toothpick spread some glue inside the beehive shape and allow to dry. This will prevent the shape from becoming concertinaed in or out, or squashed. When dry, gently spread the fringed part outwards with your fingers. Cut a sliver of red 3 cm (1 1/4") long (a 3 mm/ 1/8" paper should yield three or four slivers) and glue one end into the top of the beehive, in the hole made by the quilling tool. This is the 'style'. Do this for each flower.

ARRANGEMENT

Arrange stems as in the photograph, then add flowers as desired. The leaves are randomly placed, points up, above the flowers.

MORRISON
Verticordia nitens

Another member of the featherflower family, Morrison is a dazzling sight in full bloom. It is a summer-flowering shrub, in contrast to so many spring bloomers. The deep, rich golden-orange flowering stems can be picked and hung upside down to dry, to be used in stunning dried floral arrangements, as this flower retains its colour for years. The Latin name Verticordia is an epithet of Venus, the Turner of Hearts. Although Venus has long been identified with Aphrodite as the goddess of love, she was originally the Roman goddess of spring, and patron of flower gardens. She was worshipped by the Romans as mother of the race, and her sacred day was the first day of April.

Part	Quantity	Length	Shape	Colour
Flowers	10	20 cm (7 3/4")	strip	apricot
	10	8 cm (3 1/4")	double-fringed 10 mm (1/2") strip	yellow
	50	10 cm (4")	tight coil	apricot
Stems	1	8 cm (3 1/4")	strip	brown
	1	2 cm (3/4")	strip	brown
	1	3 cm (1 1/4")	strip	brown
Leaves	4	8 cm (3 1/4")	strip	olive green
	2	6 cm (2 1/2")	strip	olive green

To construct each flower, make a 28 cm (11") length by glueing together a 20 cm (7 3/4") apricot strip and an 8 cm (3 1/4") yellow double-fringed 10 mm (1/2") strip. Starting at the plain apricot end, roll into a beehive and glue. Remove from the quilling tool and with a toothpick spread some glue inside the beehive shape and allow to dry. When dry, gently spread the fringed part outwards with your fingers, leaving six of the fringes closest to the centre sticking up. Take five apricot tight coils and arrange them evenly around the domed centre, making sure the sticking-up fringes are in between, and then glue the tight coils on top of the spread-out fringes.

To make the leaves fold each strip in half and glue only the ends together. Bend to required shape.

ARRANGEMENT

Arrange stems first, then flowers and leaves as pictured, and glue into place.

International garden favourites

A garden is for enjoyment, and what better way to relax than to be surrounded by your favourite flowers and plants. Many of the flowers and shrubs that grow so well and prolifically in Australia are native to other parts of the world. Some, such as roses, daffodils and geraniums, are so well known that most of us don't know where they originate from. Plants migrated around the world with people as they settled in new lands, or as the early explorers took back samples of newly discovered, and to them often exotic, flora. Nowadays gardening is big business with plants shipped internationally by large companies. The quarantine regulations are quite strict in some countries so that various plant diseases don't arrive as well. Occasionally the imports love their new country so much that they run riot and become noxious weeds.

BIRD OF PARADISE
Strelitzia reginae

The Bird of Paradise is an exotic-looking plant that originates from South Africa, though the feathered birds of paradise come from New Guinea. It is a remarkably tough plant, enjoying tropical and greenhouse conditions, yet able to withstand hot dry summers in the temperate regions of the world. It is a slow grower and the young plant may not flower for several years. Flower stems can be a metre tall, and several flowers may emerge from the same stem.

Part	Quantity	Length	Shape	Colour
Flower 1	2	40 cm (15 3/4")	crescent	orange
	1	40 cm (15 3/4")	eye (squeezed flat)	orange
	1	30 cm (11 3/4")	eye (squeezed flat)	dark blue
	1	15 cm (6")	crescent	dark blue
	1	5 cm (2")	teardrop	dark blue
	1	60 cm (23 1/4")	crescent	sage green
Flower 2	1	40 cm (15 3/4")	crescent	orange
	1	40 cm (15 3/4")	eye	orange
	1	40 cm (15 3/4")	eye (squeezed flat)	orange
	1	30 cm (11 3/4")	eye (squeezed flat)	dark blue
	1	15 cm (6")	crescent	dark blue
	1	5 cm (2")	teardrop	dark blue
	1	60 cm (23 1/4")	crescent	sage green
Leaves	2	60 cm (23 1/4")	eye	sage green
	2	40 cm (15 3/4")	eye	sage green
Stems	6	assorted	strips	sage green

ARRANGEMENT

Commence by arranging flower 1 on the card, facing left. Take the 60 cm (23 1/4") green crescent and bend one end down at a 90 degree angle. Place the orange 40 cm (15 3/4") flat eye above it so it is almost parallel and one end is touching the green part near the acute bend. Place the blue 30 cm (11 3/4") flat eye above it so it is almost parallel and one end is touching the orange part where it joins on to the green. Put the blue 5 cm (2") teardrop above the blue flat eye so the pointed end touches the end that is meeting the orange part. At the other end of the blue flat eye put the 15 cm (6") blue crescent so it is pointed at the end and curves upwards. Add the two orange 40 cm (15 3/4") crescents so they are pointing upwards and touching the join between the other orange, blue and green parts.

Flower 2, facing in the opposite direction, is constructed the same way except that one of the two orange crescents pointing upwards is replaced by a 40 cm (15 3/4") orange eye.

When you are satisfied with the placement, glue flowers into place. Add the flower stems.

Position the leaves pointing upwards underneath the flowers. Add stems.

ROSE
Rosa spp.

Roses have acquired a popular and even revered status not achieved by other flowers over the centuries. Their image has been depicted in various mediums from watercolour paintings to silk ribbon embroidery. They feature on such diverse items as royal badges and postage stamps. Songs have been sung about roses and writers such as Shakespeare, Chaucer and Omar Khayyam all mentioned roses in their works. Different coloured roses mean different things, usually concerning love, and many faiths, including Buddhism, Islam, Christianity and Hinduism refer to roses. I chose to quill a yellow rose but you can use any colour you prefer.

Part	Quantity	Length	Shape	Colour
Flowers	6	20 cm (7 3/4")	10 mm (1/2") strip	yellow
Leaves	7	15 cm (6")	eye	green
	24	10 cm (4")	eye	green
Stems	1	9 cm (3 1/2")	strip	brown
	1	5 cm (2")	strip	brown
	1	3 cm (1 1/4")	strip	brown
	5	3 cm (1 1/4")	strip	green
	2	1.5 cm (5/8")	strip	green

Make the flowers following the instructions given on page 13.

ARRANGEMENT

Glue the longest of the brown stems into place and then the two shorter brown stems branching off it. Add the green leaf stems branching off the brown stems and place a large leaf at the end of each leaf stem. Position the remaining leaves in pairs either side of the leaf stem so that there are five stems with five leaves, and two stems with three leaves. Glue the flowers into place at the end of the brown stems as illustrated.

FOXGLOVE
Digitalis purpurea

A tall and domineering plant, the foxglove tends to take over the garden bed. Its fleshy leaves can smother other smaller plants growing nearby. It is rather spectacular with its long bell-shaped flowers in purple, pink and white held on tall spikes. The foxglove is a very poisonous plant, though interestingly it has medicinal qualities that are used in the treatment of heart disease. It often features in paintings of fairies.

Part	Quantity	Length	Shape	Colour
Flowers	16	15 cm (6")	10 mm (1/2") beehive	pink
	13	15 cm (6")	10 mm (1/2") beehive	white
Buds	3	9 cm (3 1/2")	teardrop	pink
	3	9 cm (3 1/2")	teardrop	white
	11	6 cm (2 1/4")	teardrop	green
Leaves	2	30 cm (11 3/4")	eye	green
	4	60 cm (23 1/4")	eye	green
Stems	2	12 cm (4 3/4")	strip	green

ARRANGEMENT

Commence by placing the two stems on the card. Add the leaves at the base. If your card is small the leaves may need to overlap. Put all the pink flowers on one stem and all the white flowers on the other. Starting from the lower part of the stem, glue on the 10 mm (1/2") beehives in pairs either side of the stem and then put a line of them on top. Add the buds.

DAFFODIL
Narcissus spp.

Daffodils are grown in gardens all over the world and are readily recognised even by people who are not botanically inclined. They are grown from a bulb which can either be dug up each year after flowering and the foliage has died back, or left in the ground for several seasons. In Greek mythology Narcissus was a handsome youth who rejected the love of the nymph Echo. He was punished for this by the gods who compelled him to fall in love with his own reflection in a pool of water. He pined away until he perished, and the flower that sprang up from where he died was named after him.

Part	Quantity	Length	Shape	Colour
Flower 1	6	30 cm (11 3/4")	eye	yellow
Stamens	3	2 cm (3/4")	10 mm (1/2") tight coil	lemon
Trumpet	1	8 cm (3 1/4")	fringed 10 mm (1/2") strip	orange or yellow
	1	8 cm (3 1/4")	8 mm (3/8") strip	orange or yellow
Flower 2	2	30 cm (11 3/4")	eye	yellow
	1	30 cm (11 3/4")	triangle	orange or yellow
Stems	1	7 cm (2 3/4")	strip	green
	1	10 cm (4")	strip	green
Leaves	1	15 cm (6")	strip	green
	1	11 cm (5 3/8")	strip	green
	1	8 cm (3 1/4")	strip	green
	1	5 cm (2")	strip	green

To make the trumpet for flower 1, take the 8 cm (3 1/4") fringed 10 mm (1/2") orange/yellow strip and the 8 cm (3 1/4") orange/yellow 8 mm (3/8") strip and glue them together to make a 16 cm (6 3/8") strip. Starting with the fringed end, roll this around a piece of dowelling approximately 2 cm (3/4") in diameter (broom handles are good). The finished cylinder should have the fringing on the inside. Glue the end while still on the dowel. When dry, gently spread the tips of the fringing outwards over the top edge of the plain strip.

To make the leaves fold each strip in half and glue together at the end only. Bend to required shape.

ARRANGEMENT

For flower 1 arrange three of the yellow eyes so they are evenly spaced and touching at their points in the centre. Glue to card. Arrange the other three yellow eyes in the same manner and place them on top of the first group to create a six-pointed star shape. Take the 3 stamens and glue them to the centre of the star so they are vertical. Place the trumpet so it encircles the stamens and glue to the star.

For flower 2, the side-view daffodil, arrange the two yellow eyes with the orange triangle in the middle so their points touch in the centre, then glue to card.

Add the stems and leaves.

COLUMBINE
Aquilegia spp.

Columbines originate from the mountain regions of America, Eurasia and Africa, and prefer a cool temperate climate. They can be grown in the shade in leafy soil or carefully nurtured in a pot on the verandah. Their flowers can be almost any colour, and the blue columbine is the state emblem of Colorado in the United States. In the world of sixteenth to eighteenth century Italian pantomime, Columbine was courted by the clownish black-masked servant Harlequin. There is also a soft caramel toffee called a columbine.

Part	Quantity	Length	Shape	Colour
Flower	1	2 cm (3/4")	10 mm (1/2") fringed strip	yellow
	5	10 cm (4")	teardrop	white
	5	20 cm (7 3/4")	teardrop	red
	1	10 cm (4")	tight coil	red

Flowers 2 and 3 are the same as flower 1.

Part	Quantity	Length	Shape	Colour
Leaf 1	5	20 cm (7 3/4")	teardrop	green

Leaves 2 and 3 are the same as leaf 1.

Part	Quantity	Length	Shape	Colour
Stems	1	10 cm (4")	strip	green
	1	8 cm (3 1/4")	strip	green
	1	6 cm (2 1/2")	strip	green
	1	2 cm (3/4")	strip	green

To make a flower, roll the 2 cm (3/4") fringed 10 mm (1/2") yellow strip into a tight coil. Glue the five white 10 cm (4") teardrops around it with their points towards the centre. Glue the five red 20 cm (7 3/4") teardrops to the red 10 cm (4") tight coil with their points facing outwards. When dry, glue the white arrangement on top of the red arrangement, so that the white teardrops appear in the gaps between the red teardrops. Make the two other flowers in the same manner.

To make a leaf glue the five green 20 cm (7 3/4") teardrops side by side to make a fan shape. Repeat for the other leaves.

ARRANGEMENT

Glue the three long stems onto the card and place a flower at the end of each one. Add the leaves and the short leaf stems.

The arid zone

Much of Australia would be classified as arid by those from Europe or the wet tropics. Here, however, I am defining 'arid' as the central part of Western Australia, which is in fact larger than the British Isles in area. This is a sparsely populated zone, and the people as well as the plants are hardy and tough. Once the domain of indigenous peoples and pastoralists, the region is now heavily explored by both mining companies and tourists. The ecostructure of these arid areas is fragile, and overgrazing, drought, flood and fire have all taken their toll. Fortunately, with conservation becoming an important item on the political agenda, nowadays there is a lot of research and work being done with revegetation in ravaged areas, stocking rates are more realistic, and new commercial horticultural projects are being launched.

RUBY SALTBUSH
Enchylaena tomentosa

Ornamental as well as edible, the Ruby Saltbush is popular with outback stock as a delicious juicy alternative to boring dry grasses. Birds also enjoy the fruits. It grows in virtually all soil types and plays a valuable role in the revegetation of mine sites and denuded pastoral lands. An abundance of mature Ruby Saltbush plants is a good indicator that the area is in a healthy condition. Despite the name, the plant in fact contains only 6 per cent salt and is much more palatable than many other succulents.

Part	Quantity	Length	Shape	Colour
Fruits	24	10 cm (4")	tight coil	red
Stems	5	assorted	strip	brown
Leaves	81	5 cm (2")	teardrop	sage green

ARRANGEMENT

Position three main stems (say 8 –11 cm / 3 1/4 - 4 1/4") with two shorter stems (say 3–4 cm / 1 1/4 - 1 1/2") branching off them. Glue leaves and fruit randomly along each side of the stems until they are completely covered.

TALL MULLA-MULLA
Ptilotus exaltatus

Stranded in the desert? Fancy a fresh green salad? No, it is not a mirage. Look no further than the broad leaves of this species of mulla-mulla. Personally speaking I prefer hot cooked vegetables, but if it was a matter of survival I suppose there could be worse things on the menu. Besides, millions of sheep and kangaroos can't be wrong. They adore the stuff. Oh, and the flowers aren't bad looking either!

Part	Quantity	Length	Shape	Colour
Flowers	6	26 cm (10 1/4")	fringed 10 mm (1/2") strip	purple
	6	26 cm (10 1/4")	fringed 10 mm (1/2") strip	white
Stems	6	assorted	strip	green
Leaves	2	20 cm (7 3/4")	eye	green
	2	15 cm (6")	leaf	green
	2	10 cm (4")	leaf	green
	2	8 cm (3 1/4")	leaf	green

To make each flower take a strip of fringed purple and a strip of fringed white and roll them together to make a beehive, making sure that the white is on the outside. Remove carefully from the quilling tool and with a toothpick spread glue inside the beehive to help maintain its shape. When dry, gently spread out the fringes until the shape resembles a pine cone.

ARRANGEMENT

Position stems as desired and glue to card. Place a flower on its side (you may need to flatten the fringes on this side a bit) at the top of each stem. Take the two 20 cm (7 3/4") green eyes and glue them at the base of the plant. Arrange the remaining leaves, one on each stem.

DESERT KURRAJONG
Brachychiton gregorii

The little people of Lilliput would have marvelled at these ready-made boats, the seed-pods of the Desert Kurrajong, although it is a long way to the sea from where this tree grows, and lakes with water in them are also in short supply. The bright green foliage of the Desert Kurrajong is a welcome contrast to the drabness of the surrounding scrub, making them easily identified in a sea of grey. Kurrajongs are loners, with single trees located kilometres apart, a characteristic in keeping with the solitary lifestyle of the human population around this part of the world.

Part	Quantity	Length	Shape	Colour
Seed pods	7	60 cm (23 1/4")	beehive	black
Seeds	35	5 cm (2")	tight coil	apricot
Stems	1	11 cm (4 1/4")	strip	brown
	1	5 cm (2")	strip	brown
	4	assorted	strip	lemon
	7	1 cm (1/2")	strip	black
Leaves	4	50 cm (19 3/4")	birdfoot	green

To make the seed pods, take each 60 cm (23 1/4") beehive and squeeze it into an eye. Flatten it until it resembles a shallow boat. Spread glue inside so it will keep its shape, and place several seeds inside.

ARRANGEMENT

Arrange the two brown stems to hang down from the top of the card. At the end of each position the short black stems, radiating outwards. Put a seed pod at the end of each black stem. Add the lemon stems branching off the brown stems, and place a leaf at the end of each one, hanging down.

WILD TOMATO
Solanum orbiculatum

The Solanum family, whose members are spread worldwide, contains many useful plants such as the potato, tomato and capsicum. It also contains some of the most toxic plants such as Deadly Nightshade, Thornapple and Pituri. One member of the family that used to be in the 'useful' list but would nowadays most likely be included under the 'toxic' heading is the tobacco plant. Wild Tomato is not a particularly user-friendly shrub as it has rather long strong spines along the stems. It may or may not be toxic, but stock don't appear to eat it, if that's any indication. It does hold the soil together though!

Part	Quantity	Length	Shape	Colour
Flowers	20	1 cm (1/2")	10 mm (1/2") tight coil	yellow
	20	12 cm (4 3/4")	eye	deep mauve
Stems	2	8 cm (3 1/4")	strip	sage green
	2	2 cm (3/4")	strip	sage green
Leaves	11	15 cm (6")	teardrop	sage green
	2	12 cm (4 3/4")	teardrop	sage green

Each of the four flowers is constructed with five 10 mm (1/2") yellow tight coils in the centre, surrounded by five deep mauve eyes.

ARRANGEMENT
Place stems into position and glue to card. Put a flower at the end of each stem. Add leaves.

Terrestrial orchids

Worldwide, the orchid family contains 25 000 species. They can be found all over the world barring the deserts and polar regions. In Australia alone there are over 900 species. Tropical regions can claim more than half of these, the epiphytes or air plants. Terrestrial orchids grow in the soil on the ground, and Western Australia has a larger number of species of this type than any other state. There is even a species that lives and flowers entirely underground. Its discovery came about quite by accident in 1928 when it was uncovered by a farmer ploughing his paddock.

Terrestrial orchids are a passion with many people of all ages, some of whom will travel hundreds of kilometres each year seeking out known locations of individual specimens. There is always the hope of finding a rare or hitherto unknown species to add to the records, not to mention the thrill of simply being able to find such a tiny plant amongst hectares of sometimes quite dense scrub and tall grasses.

BLUE LADY ORCHID
Thelymitra crinita

I had the opportunity to see the Blue Lady Orchid in the wild one spring and it was simply magnificent. It was much taller then I had realised (over knee high) and the flowers were the most incredible shade of blue. I had a camera with me and used up the entire film. I returned later in the afternoon with fresh film to find that the flowers were all closed up ready for bed! I knew they were light sensitive, but hadn't realised just how much, as it was still only mid-afternoon. Fortunately they were out bright and early the next morning and I was able to snap away to my heart's content.

Part	Quantity	Length	Shape	Colour
Flower 1	1	5 cm (2")	tight coil	yellow
	1	15 cm (6")	beehive	blue
	2	15 cm (6")	teardrop	blue
	4	15 cm (6")	eye	blue

Flower 2 is made the same way as flower 1.

Part	Quantity	Length	Shape	Colour
Stems	1	7 cm (2 3/4")	strip	sage green
	2	3 cm (1 1/4")	strip	sage green
	2	0.5 cm (1/4")	strip	sage green
Buds	2	15 cm (6")	teardrop	sage green
	1	20 cm (7 3/4")	teardrop	sage green

ARRANGEMENT

To make the first flower, position the beehive in the centre so it looks like a cup. Arrange the blue teardrops and eyes around the centre (see photograph). Glue into position on the card. Place the yellow tight coil next to and above the blue beehive and glue into place. Make the second flower. Add the stems, and lastly the buds.

JUG ORCHID
Pterostylis recurva

Greenhood orchids are recognised by the hooded appearance of their mainly green flowers. The hood of the species known as the Jug Orchid is inverted, giving it quite a different and remarkable appearance. The flowers still retain the typical green and white striped look, though when almost finished they can have quite a reddish-bronze tinge to them. Jug Orchids are the tallest of the greenhoods, their flowers sometimes peeking through the lowest foliage of other shrubs, and they can have up to four flowers per stem. They are mainly distributed through the south-west of Western Australia.

Part	Quantity	Length	Shape	Colour
Flower 1	1	22 cm (8 3/4")	strip	olive green
	1	21 cm (8 1/4")	strip	white
	1	15 cm (6")	strip	olive green
	1	14 cm (5 1/2")	strip	white
	1	1 cm (1/2")	strip	olive green
Flowers 2 and 3 are the same as flower 1.				
Stems	1	10 cm (4")	strip	olive green
	2	2 cm (3/4")	strip	olive green
Leaves	4	12 cm (4 3/4")	teardrop	olive green

To make the flower take the 15 cm (6") olive-green and 14 cm (5 1/2")white strips and roll together to make a loose coil. Make sure the olive-green is on the outside. Squeeze coil into a bent teardrop. Do the same with the 22 cm (8 3/4") olive-green and 21 cm (8 1/4") white strip, but shape this loose coil into a leaf. Attach the 1 cm (1/2") olive-green strip to the end of the leaf shape at a right angle.

ARRANGEMENT

Following the photograph, position and glue the stems on the card. Add the flowers, and then the leaves.

QUEEN OF SHEBA
Thelymitra variegata

Legends abound about the Queen of Sheba, her wealth and splendour, her gorgeous cavalcade to Jerusalem to meet King Solomon. Tales of his magnificence and wisdom had spread throughout the East and the Queen wanted to check it out for herself. After Solomon successfully answered all her questions the Queen gave him an enormous amount of gold, jewels and spices. Solomon in turn gave her everything she asked for, and she went back home. Ethiopian legend has it that she bore him a son on her return journey. Arab legend married her to Solomon (in addition to his other 300 wives), and said that after her death he buried her in a magnificent tomb in Palmyra.

Part	Quantity	Length	Shape	Colour
Flower 1	2	15 cm (6")	bent teardrop	purple
	1	15 cm (6")	eye	purple
	1	5 cm (2")	strip	purple
	1	5 cm (2")	strip	red
	4	5 cm (2")	strip	yellow
	2	10 cm (4")	strip	red
	1	10 cm (4")	strip	purple
	1	1 cm (1/2")	6 mm (1/4") strip	purple
	3	5 cm (2")	crescent	yellow

Flowers 2 and 3 are the same as flower 1.

Stems	1	6 cm (2 1/2")	strip	green
	2	2 cm (3/4")	strip	green

Firstly create the flower centre. Take a 5 cm (2") yellow strip, a 10 cm (4") purple strip and a 1 cm (1/2") purple 6 mm (1/4") strip, and join them together with glue to make a 16 cm (6 3/8") strip. Starting at the yellow end, roll into a beehive.

The multi-coloured petals are next. Make a three-colour 15 cm (6") strip by joining together a 5 cm (2") purple strip, a 5 cm (2") red strip and a 5 cm (2") yellow strip. Starting at the purple end, roll into a loose coil. Shape it into an eye.

Take a 10 cm (4") red strip and join it to a 5 cm (2") yellow strip to make a two-colour 15 cm (6") strip. Starting at the red end, roll it into a loose coil. Shape it into an eye. Make two of these.

ARRANGEMENT

I found it easier to put the flowers in place first, and then cut the stems to fit between them. Place the flower centre into position, making sure the wide strip section is at the top, rather like a mudguard over a wheel. Arrange the petals around it, clockwise from the top: the three-colour eye, a purple bent teardrop, a two-colour eye, the purple eye, another two-colour eye, another purple bent teardrop.

Take the three yellow crescents and glue them to the centre, on the wide purple section, one bending down and two bending up like horns.

Arrange the remaining flowers in the same manner and then join them together with the stems. Refer to the photograph if still in doubt!

YELLOW CHINA ORCHID
Cyanicula ixioides subsp. ixioides

Cyaniculas are a genus of blue-flowering orchids, taking their name from kyanos, Greek for blue. This is the only member of the genus that is not blue, which makes it a bit of an oddity, and has given it a somewhat confused history since being described by the botanist John Lindley in 1840. Lindley, born near Norwich, England, in 1799, was the author of many scientific and popular publications on botany as well as lecturing on the subject at the Royal Institution and the Chelsea Botanic Gardens. He died of apoplexy in 1865.

Part	Quantity	Length	Shape	Colour
Flowers	15	15 cm (6")	eye	yellow
	6	5 cm (2")	crescent	lemon
Stems	1	5 cm (2")	strip	green
	2	3 cm (1 1/4")	strip	green
Leaves	2	15 cm (6")	teardrop	green

ARRANGEMENT

Each flower is made up of five yellow eyes, which are the petals, and two lemon crescents that form the centre. Turn the crescent shapes on end and glue one on top of the other, piggy-back style. Still on end, glue into position on the card. Arrange the five yellow eyes evenly around the centre and glue into place. Do the same with the remaining flowers. Add stems, and finally the leaves.

Ground huggers

Ground-hugging plants can vary from small mats to spreading carpets, from scattered low-growing individuals to dense, sprawling, prostrate shrubs. Many plants are ideal as ground and rockery covers. They play an important role in preserving moisture by reducing evaporation from the soil, and preventing erosion from wind and rain. They discourage weeds, and keep the temperature of the soil down. Their role in the ecostructure is as important as that of the tallest gum tree. These low plants provide a cool canopy for crawling insects which in turn are a source of food for many birds. Their varied flowers attract the eye downwards, proving that you don't have to be tall to be noticed!

PINCUSHIONS
Borya constricta

Pincushions are a useful sewing aid, a small cushion firmly filled with wadding into which pins are inserted, ready for use. When in flower, this ground cover resembles a green cushion full of white-headed pins. The leaves are in fact as spiky as pins too, if you should happen to kneel on one. During the summer the tufts appear dead but after rain they turn orange and then green in a remarkably short time. Flowering occurs during spring. *Borya constricta* is not to be confused with the serpent of a similar Latin name!

Part	Quantity	Length	Shape	Colour
Flowers	9	9 cm (3 1/2")	fringed 6 mm (1/4") strip	white
Stems	6	4 cm (1 1/2")	strip	light-green
	2	3 cm (1 1/4")	strip	light-green
	1	2 cm (3/4")	strip	light-green
Leaves	11	26 cm (10 1/4")	fringed 10 mm (1/2") strip	green

Both flowers and leaves are formed in the same way. Roll each fringed length into a tight coil and glue. When dry, spread out the fringes.

ARRANGEMENT

Position all the leaves into an attractive clump. Arrange stems sticking up and out from the clump, and place a flower at the tip of each stem.

HAIRY LESCHENAULTIA
Leschenaultia hirsuta

The 26 species of Leschenaultia occur only in Australia—and 20 of them are to be found in Western Australia. Leschenaultias bloom in a myriad of colours, from the palest to the deepest of blues, creamy white, vivid scarlet, bright crimson, soft pink, sunny yellow and glowing orange. Several are bicoloured. This particular species has flowers of the most intense red, and prefers to grow in sandy soil.

Part	Quantity	Length	Shape	Colour
Flowers	24	20 cm (7 3/4)	arrow	red
	6	7 cm (2 3/4")	bent teardrop	red
Stems	1	8 cm (3 1/4")	strip	dark green
	1	6 cm (2 1/2")	strip	dark green
	2	5 cm (2")	strip	dark green
	1	3 cm (1 1/4")	strip	dark green
	2	1 cm (1/2")	strip	dark green
Leaves	5	4 cm (1 1/2")	strip	dark green
	3	2 cm (3/4")	strip	dark green

ARRANGEMENT

Each flower is made of four red arrows, arranged with points touching in the centre. One arrow is upright and the remaining three fan out below like a skirt. Take a red bent teardrop shape and turn it on end. Glue the bent end to the centre of the flower so the fat end juts out like a beak. Arrange and glue all six flowers into the desired position. Add stems.

To make the leaves fold each strip in half and glue together at the end only. Bend slightly to the required shape and glue into position.

VIOLA
Viola tricolor

I always have difficulty in working out the differences between a viola and a pansy. They are both members of the same family and, indeed, this particular species of viola is the ancestor of the modern pansy. Pansies are much showier with colourful blotched petals, occasionally frilled around the edges. The viola is more subdued and subtle in both colour and size. Flowers can be all one colour, either mauve or yellow, or a combination, as is this species. Violas are popular as border plants and will also do well in outdoor containers.

Part	Quantity	Length	Shape	Colour
Flower 1	2	15 cm (6")	teardrop	purple
	2	15 cm (6")	teardrop	yellow
	1	20 cm (7 3/4")	teardrop	yellow
	1	5 cm (2")	crescent	white
	1	5 cm (2")	tight coil	yellow
Flowers 2, 3, 4 and 5 are the same as flower 1.				
Leaves	1	40 cm (15 3/4")	eye	green
	1	20 cm (7 3/4")	eye	green
	2	30 cm (11 3/4")	eye	green
	2	35 cm (13 3/4")	eye	green
Main stem	1	10 cm (4")	strip	green
Short stems	4	assorted	strip	green

ARRANGEMENT

Arrange the flowers as in the photograph, glueing the purple and yellow teardrops with their points all touching in the centre, to the card. Glue the 5 cm (2") yellow tight coil to the inside curve of the 5 cm (2") white crescent, and then glue it on top of the centre of the viola. Add stems and leaves.

LILY OF THE VALLEY
Convallaria majalis

The flowers of this delicate little plant hang off the stems like little bells and their perfume is delicious. Lily of the Valley is essentially a cold climate plant, which thrives in the native forests of France, Siberia and Canada. A tiny plant, it was very popular in pioneer gardens despite a superstition that it was unlucky to plant it, and today is grown worldwide.

Part	Quantity	Length	Shape	Colour
Flowers	17	30 cm (11 3/4")	beehive	white
Leaves	1	60 cm (23 1/4")	leaf	green
	1	120 cm (46 1/2")	leaf	green
Stems	1	10 cm (4")	strip	green
	1	9 cm (3 1/2")	strip	green
	13	4 mm (3/16")	strip	white

ARRANGEMENT

Position the two long stems on the card and place a leaf on either side, touching at the base. Put the 4 mm (3/16") white stems branching out and down along the long stems. Place a flower at the end of each short stem. The extra flowers can be added on top of the long stems.

BOOMERANG TRIGGERPLANT
Stylidium breviscapum subsp. erythrocalyx

My boomerang won't come back! A plaintive cry that accompanies the beginning efforts of all would-be boomerang throwers. Aborigines carved these curved implements from wood for use as hunting weapons, and although we always think of them all as returning to the thrower, in fact only one type of boomerang was designed in this manner. They are a popular artefact with tourists, and a range of plastic 'trick' boomerangs is sold in toy stores. It is fairly easy to see how this species of triggerplant came by its common name, the two curved petals closely resembling the shape of a boomerang. Non-returning no doubt!

Part	Quantity	Length	Shape	Colour
Flower 1	1	5 cm (2")	tight coil	lemon
	1	1 cm (1/2")	strip	lemon
	4	1 cm (1/2")	tight coil	red
	2	10 cm (4")	teardrop	white
	2	20 cm (7 3/4")	bent teardrop	white

Flowers 2, 3 and 4 are the same as flower 1.

Part	Quantity	Length	Shape	Colour
Leaves	6	20 cm (7 3/4")	eye	green
	9	15 cm (6")	eye	green

Take the 1 cm (1/2") lemon strip and cut it in half lengthways. Glue one of these thin strips to the lemon tight coil so it is sticking up, then bend it over a bit. This is the centre of the flower, the 'trigger'. Glue into position on the card.

Take the two white teardrops and the two white bent teardrops and glue them around the centre as in the photograph. Add the four red tight coils, putting one inside the pointed end of each of the white teardrop petals.

Repeat this procedure for the rest of the flowers.

ARRANGEMENT

Glue the flowers into position first. Squeeze the leaves firmly until they are almost flat, then glue them into position, making sure they stay in their flattened shape.

BLACK TOOTHBRUSHES
Grevillea hookeriana

Imagine cleaning your teeth with one of these! The name *Grevillea* commemorates Charles Francis Greville, a vice-president of the Royal Horticultural Society of London, instituted in 1804 for the improvement of horticulture. There are 340 species of *Grevillea* in Australia. Their flowers come in different forms and are variously described as spider-like, snail-like, toothbrush-shaped, lantern-shaped and grape-like, as well as being in plumes or spikes. Owing to the large amounts of nectar they produce, grevilleas are a great attraction to a variety of birds.

Part	Quantity	Length	Shape	Colour
Flowers	10	10 cm (4")	loose coil	light green
	10	2 cm (3/4")	strip	black
	3	2 cm (3/4")	tight coil	black
Stems	2	8 cm (3 1/4")	strip	mid-green
Leaves	9	4 cm (1 1/2")	strip	mid-green

To form the flowers make teardrop shapes from the light green loose coils. Then take the pinched end of each teardrop, put it in the slot of the quilling tool, and roll it half a turn. This will make it very curved on the end.

ARRANGEMENT

Gently curve the two stems and glue them into position. Take five of the light green flowers and arrange them in line on one side of the first stem at the end, as shown in the photograph. Do the same with the other five flowers on the second stem. Take a black strip and attach it to the last flower on stem 1, adding a black tight coil at the tip. Repeat this for two flowers on stem 2. Take the remaining black strips, bend them into upside-down U-shapes and attach over the top of the remaining flowers on each stem. Finally add curved green strips for leaves along each stem.

Indoor and container dwellers

Many people who enjoy gardening are restricted in the amount of time or energy they can devote to a garden because of where they live or because of ill health. Container gardening is ideal for the city dweller in high rise apartments, busy professionals who don't have much time in between working hours, and people who no longer have the physical strength to maintain a large traditional garden. Modern containers are varied in size, colour and shape and in the material from which they are made, ranging from terracotta and concrete to wood, plastic and wire. They can stand on the ground or hang from overhead. Container gardens can be established indoors in a kitchen or bathroom, outdoors on verandahs, balconies, courtyards and patios, and in greenhouses and shadehouses. Whatever your need or situation you will be able to find suitable plants and containers.

CYCLAMEN
Cyclamen hederifolium

Cyclamens originate from the alpine woodlands of Palestine, Asia Minor and the eastern end of the Mediterranean. They are suitable for growing outdoors in cold climates, but in many warmer countries are prized as a winter-flowering pot plant. The flowers are unusual in that their petals all curve upwards, rather like an umbrella blown inside out in a strong wind. The leaves too are rather striking with their rich blend of dark green and silvery grey-green.

Part	Quantity	Length	Shape	Colour
Flower 1	3	10 cm (4")	eye	pink, white, mauve or red
	1	1 cm (1/2")	strip	pink, white, mauve or red
Flowers 2, 3, 4 and 5 are the same as flower 1.				
Large leaves	2	10 cm (4")	strip	dark green
	2	15 cm (6")	strip	light green
	2	20 cm (7 3/4")	strip	dark green
Small leaves	2	5 cm (2")	strip	dark green
	2	10 cm (4")	strip	light green
	2	15 cm (6")	strip	dark green
Stems	9	assorted	strip	brown

To make a large leaf, join together end to end one of each of the green strips to make a 45 cm (17 3/4") strip—first the 10 cm (4") dark green strip, then the 15 cm (6") light green strip, and last the 20 cm (7 3/4") dark green strip. Roll into a loose coil, starting from the 10 cm (4") dark green end, which you then squeeze into an arrow shape. Pinch two extra points into each side of the arrow to give a rough-edged look to the leaf. Do the same for the other large leaf and the two smaller leaves.

ARRANGEMENT

To make the flowers, glue the 1 cm (1/2") strips horizontally on your card in the positions the flowers are required. Glue three eyes side by side so that one point of each is touching the strip and the other is pointing upwards. Add stems to suit. Place leaves in position and add their stems.

PEACE LILY
Spathiphyllum spp.

Spathiphyllums are among the hardiest and most popular indoor plants, grown throughout the world. They don't mind being over-watered, and cope well with the dry air often associated with air-conditioning in offices and airports. In the tropics they grow superbly outdoors as well. The flowers last for ages on the plant, but if you cut them to put in a vase they droop within minutes! The name Peace Lily is reckoned to date from the hippie era of the 1960s.

Part	Quantity	Length	Shape	Colour
FLOWER 1				
Spathe	1	60 cm (23 1/4")	teardrop	white
Spadix	5	15 cm (6")	tight coil	cream
	10	4 cm (1 1/2")	tight coil	cream
Flowers 2 and 3 are the same as flower 1.				
Leaves	6	30 cm (11 3/4")	eye	green
Stems	9	assorted	strip	green

To make the spadix glue the five 15 cm (6") cream tight coils on top of each other, as shown in the photograph. Glue one of the 4 cm (1 1/2") tight coils on top. Glue the remaining nine tight coils to the sides in three rows of three. Make two more the same way.

ARRANGEMENT

Arrange the white flower spathes on the card as desired and glue on. Place one spadix centrally on top of each spathe so that their bases are level, and glue into place. Add stems to flowers. Arrange leaves so they are below the flowers. Glue them on and add stems to suit.

WATER LILY
Nymphaea spp.

Whenever I think of water lilies I imagine frogs sitting on the lily pads, and goldfish swimming casually underneath in the water. There is something very tranquil and calming about water gardening, which can be done on a large scale in a pond, or on a miniature scale in a container. Water lilies float regally on the surface of the water, with no visible connection to soil or roots. Water lilies are primeval plants whose ancestors grew in the drinking water of the dinosaurs, and they appeared in paintings in ancient Egyptian temples. They come in a myriad of colours—yellow, pink, lilac, white, blue and red.

Part	Quantity	Length	Shape	Colour
Flower 1	20	15 cm (6")	eye	yellow
	1	40 cm (15 3/4")	tight coil	yellow
	1	20 cm (7 3/4")	tight coil	yellow
			fringed 10 mm (1/2")	

Flowers 2 and 3 are the same as flower 1 but made in pink and lilac.

Lily pads	2	40 cm (15 3/4")	loose coils	green
	2	20 cm (7 3/4")	loose coils	green
	4	30 cm (11 3/4")	loose coils	green

Construct the flower before placing it on the card. Take ten of the 15 cm (6") eyes and the 40 cm (15 3/4") tight coil. With the coil in the centre, glue the eyes around it to make a ten-point star shape. Take the remaining ten eyes and the fringed tight coil and make another ten-point star. Place the star shape with the fringed centre on top of the other star shape so the points are offset, and glue together. Fan out the fringes slightly.

ARRANGEMENT

Glue the water lily flowers and lily pads onto your card in the desired positions.

IVY-LEAF GERANIUM
Pelargonium peltatum

Mention the word geranium and I immediately imagine a Mediterranean balcony with terracotta pots and wooden window boxes spilling over with glorious geraniums in a riot of colour. In fact the geranium's country of origin is South Africa. The Ivy-Leaf Geranium is a trailing plant which can be trained up on a trellis or left to cascade from a hanging basket. It can also be used as a ground cover. Flowers come in a variety of shades of red, pink, white and mauve, and I have recently seen a specimen that was a velvety plum colour.

Part	Quantity	Length	Shape	Colour
Flower 1	1	1 cm (1/2")	10 mm (1/2") fringed strip	red, pink or white
	5	10 cm (4")	teardrop	red, pink or white
Flowers 2, 3, 4 and 5 are the same as flower 1.				
Leaves	2	20 cm (7 3/4")	star	green
	4	25 cm (9 3/4")	star	green
Buds	6	4 cm (1 1/2")	eye	green
Stems	10	assorted	strip	green

To make the flower centres roll the 1 cm (1/2") fringed strip of the chosen colour into a tight coil.

ARRANGEMENT

Begin by glueing the flower centres to the card. Then arrange five teardrops of the same colour around the centres so that the two top teardrops are slightly separated from the three bottom teardrops. Glue the six green buds in a group 1 cm (1/2") below the lowest flower. Place one stem going down from the buds to the bottom of the card. Place three short stems going up from the buds to the three lowest flowers. Add two main leaf stems and put a leaf at the end of each. Add remaining leaves on short stems branching off the main leaf stems.

CINERARIA
Senecio cruentus

Cinerarias originate from the Canary Islands. They are fairly fussy in regard to climate, preferring the temperature to be not too hot, not too cold, but just right. Rather like Goldilocks and the porridge! The plants do well in containers and a massed mix of potted blooms makes a spectacular display. Cinerarias are an annual plant, and the best flowering results come from fresh plantings each year.

Part	Quantity	Length	Shape	Colour
Flower group 1	6	5 cm (2")	strip	dark pink
	6	5 cm (2")	6 mm (1/4") fringed strip	white
	6	8 cm (3 1/4")	10 mm (1/2") fringed strip	dark pink
Flower group 2	3	10 cm (4")	strip	dark blue
	3	5 cm (2")	10 mm (1/2") fringed strip	white
Flower group 3	5	10 cm (4")	strip	violet
	5	5 cm (2")	10 mm (1/2") fringed strip	pink
Flower group 4	4	10 cm (4")	strip	dark pink
	4	5 cm (2")	10 mm (1/2") fringed strip	mauve
Flower group 5	4	5 cm (2")	strip	white
	4	5 cm (2")	strip	dark blue
	4	8 cm (3 1/4")	10 mm (1/2") fringed strip	light blue
Flower group 6	4	5 cm (2")	strip	dark blue
	4	5 cm (2")	6 mm (1/4") fringed strip	white
	4	8 cm (3 1/4")	10 mm (1/2") fringed strip	light blue
Leaves	11	10 cm (4")	arrow	green
	9	20 cm (7 3/4")	arrow	green
Planter box	11	20 cm (7 3/4")	eye	brown

Make the fringed flowers in their colour groups, joining together end to end the plain and fringed strips to make a long strip. Commencing at the plain end, roll the long strip into a tight coil and glue. When dry, gently spread out the fringes. You should have 26 flowers altogether.

ARRANGEMENT

Start by making the planter box. Glue nine of the brown eyes vertically side by side across near the base of the card. Put the remaining two eyes underneath for the legs. Glue on the flowers in their colour groups. Add the leaves randomly.

Further reading

Corrick, M.G., Furer, B. & George, A.S. (1996): *Wildflowers of Southern Western Australia*, The Five Mile Press, Noble Park, Victoria

Erickson, R., George, A.S., Marchant, N.G. & Morcombe, M.K. (1988): *Flowers and Plants of Western Australia*, Reed Books, Sydney

Gardner, C.A. (1975): *Wildflowers of Western Australia*, 12th edn, West Australian Newspapers, Perth

Hoffman, N. & Brown, A.P. (1992): *Orchids of South West Australia*, 2nd edn, University of Western Australia Press, Perth

Keighery, G. (1996): *Common Wildflowers of the Mid-West*, Department of Conservation and Land Management, Perth

Mann, R. (1995): *The Ultimate Book of Flowers for Australian Gardeners*, Mynah, Sydney

Mitchell, A.A. & Wilcox D.G. (1994): *Arid Shrubland Plants*, 2nd edn, University of Western Australia Press, Perth

Morris, M. (1991): *Quilling*, Regal Publications, Launceston

Walter, H. (1998): *Quilling Western Australian Wildflowers*, Kangaroo Press, Sydney

Woolston-Hamey, J. (1995): *Quilling Australian Native Flowers*, Kangaroo Press, Sydney